THE
BEST
JOKE
BOOK
FOR
Silly
KIDS

What do you call a penguin in the
Sahara Desert?
Lost!

What do you call a train filled with
toffee?
A *chew chew* train!

Dad, can you put my shoes on?
No, I don't think they'll fit me!

How did the human cannonball lose
his job?
He got fired!

Why does a baker bake bread?
Because he kneads the dough!

Which type of dog has no tail?
A hotdog!

Why can't a leopard hide?

Because they are always spotted!

I'll call you later.
Don't call me later, call me *Dad!*

Why do pens get sent to prison?
To do long sentences!

What did the girl say to her father
when he fell in the river?
Paddle, pop!

Hear the joke about the wall?
I can't get over it....

What did the mama cow say to the
baby cow?
It's *pasture* bedtime!

Why can't you hear a pterodactyl using the bathroom?

Because the P is silent!

Knock Knock

Who's there?

Robin.

Robin who?

Robbing you, give me your money!

Why didn't the skeleton go to the party?
He had *no-body* to go with!

What do snowmen call their kids?
Chill-dren!

What is green and sits in the corner?
A naughty frog!

What do you call a crazy golfer?
A crack putt!

What lies in a pram and wobbles?
A jelly baby!

Who invented fractions?
Henry the 1/8th!

Would You Rather:

...travel through space on a skateboard
-or-
travel through time on a jet ski?

What do they sing at a snowman's
birthday party?
Freeze a jolly good fellow!

How do monkeys make toast?
**They stick some bread under the
gorilla!**

What does the carpet salesman
give to his wife for
Valentine's Day?
Rugs and kisses!

What kind of room has no
windows or doors?
A mushroom!

What do you call cattle with a sense of humor?
Laughing stock!

What's the best thing about being 103 years old?
No peer pressure!

Why did the scientist install a knocker on his door?
He wanted to win the no-bell prize!

Who delivers presents to dogs?
Santa Paws!

How do you hire a horse?
Stand it on four bricks!

'Without geometry life is pointless!'

What do you get if you cross a skeleton with a detective?
Sherlock Bones!

What do you get if you cross a stereo with a refrigerator?
Cool music!

Who says, "oh, oh, oh"?
Santa walking backwards!

What do you get if you cross a bell with a skunk?
Jingle Smells!

What do you call two robbers?
A pair of knickers!

What do you call a deer with no eyes?
eyes?
No idea!

What do you call a deer with no eyes *and* no legs?
Still no idea!

Knock knock.
Who's there?
Cash.
Cash who?
No thanks, but I'll have some peanuts.

What do you get if you cross a
chicken with a cement mixer?
A brick-layer!

Why do grasshoppers not go to
football matches?
They prefer cricket matches!

What are the small rivers that run
into the Nile?
The juve-niles!

How did the Vikings send secret
messages?
By Norse code!

Would You Rather:

...run with scissors blindfolded

-or-

run around an active volcano?

What do hedgehogs eat?
Prickled onions!

Why does a spider bring toilet
paper to a party?
Because he is a party pooper!

How do bubbles communicate?
By mobile foam!

Why are skeletons so calm?
Because nothing gets under their
skin!

What's Tarzan's favorite song?
Jungle Bells!

Why do scuba divers fall backwards into the water?
If they fell forwards they'd still be in the boat!

What do vampires sing on New Year's Eve?
Auld *Fang* Syne!

What's the fastest thing in water?
A motor pike!

What do you get if you cross a cowboy with an octopus?
Billy the Squid!

Knock knock.

Who's there?

Boo.

Boo who?

No need to cry, it's only a joke.

Knock knock.

Who's there?

Lettuce.

Lettuce who?

Lettuce in, it's cold out here!

Knock knock.

Who's there?

Alien

Alien who?

What?– how many extra-terrestrials do
you know?

Why is Europe like a frying pan?
Because it has *Greece* at the
bottom!

What do you call an elephant that
never washes?
A smellyphant!

How does a snowman travel
around?
By riding an icicle!

Where do snow-women like to
dance?
At snowballs!

What do snowmen wear on their heads?
heads?
Ice caps!

Why was the snowman looking through
through
the carrots?
He was picking his nose!

Why does it take pirates so long to learn the alphabet?
to learn the alphabet?
Because they can spend years at c!

A man walks into a bar ....**ouch!**

What is black and white and noisy?
A zebra with a drum kit!

Why did the man get the sack
from the orange juice factory?
Because he couldn't concentrate!

Why did the mechanic sleep under
the car?
He wanted to get up *oily* in the
morning!

How do you make a bandstand?
Hide all the chairs!

What do you get when you cross a
sheep with a kangaroo?
A woolly jumper!

What happens when you throw a stone into the red sea?
It gets wet.

What's white and dangerous?
A fridge falling out of the sky!

What do you call a man with no nose and no body?
Nobody nose!

I cut my finger chopping cheese, but I think that I may have *grater* problems!

Which animal talks the most?
A yak!

What do you call a man with a pole
in his leg?
Rod-ney!

What do you call a snowman in the summer time?
A puddle!

What is the best present you can receive?
A broken drum. You can't beat it!

What did Adam say the day before Christmas?
It's Christmas, Eve!

What table at school doesn't have legs?
The multiplication table!

What's brown and sticky?
A stick!

What's black and white and eats
like a horse?
A zebra!

What type of fish is the most
famous?
A starfish!

How many golfers does it take to
change a lightbulb?
Fore!

"Hey, did you get a haircut?"
"No, I got them *all* cut."

What's red and white?
Pink!

What do you call a boomerang
that does not come back?
A stick!

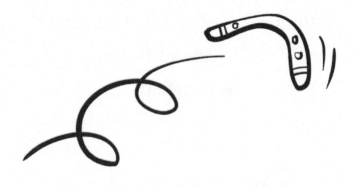

What do you call a man lying under
a car?
Jack!

What do you call a man with a shovel?
Doug!

What do you call a man *without* a shovel?
Douglas!

What do you call a man in a pile of leaves?
Russell!

What do you call a lady with one leg?
Ilene!

What do you call a man with no arms and no legs lying in front of your door?

Matt!

Why was the kangaroo mad at her children?

Because they ate biscuits in bed!

Why did the tomato blush?

Because he saw the salad dressing!

What does Dracula take when he's sick?

Coffin syrup!

Did you know?

The human body has over 600 muscles!

An elephant can produce a 7 gallon pile of poop! Ewww!

What did Dad spider say to baby spider?
You spend too much time on the web!

What do you call a group of killer whales playing instruments?
An orca-stra!

What sort of animal needs oil?
Mice, because they squeak!

How long does it take a candle to burn?
About a wick!

How do hedgehogs kiss?
Very carefully!

Why did the tightrope walker go to
his bank?
To check his balance!

How do you start a teddy bear
race?
Teddy, Set, Go!

What do you call a line of men waiting for a haircut?
A barber-queue!

What sort of TV program do ducks watch?
Duckumentaries!

Why do crabs never give to charity?
Because they're shellfish!

What kind of magic do cows believe in?
MOODOO!

What time is it?

I don't know. It keeps changing!

What is blue and smells like red paint?

Blue paint!

What's a chicken's favorite vegetable?

Eggplant!

Dad, how do I look?

With your eyes!

What do clouds wear?
Thunderwear!

What invention lets you see
through walls?
Windows!

What was the tortoise doing on the freeway?
About 1 mile per hour!

How did the man drown in his bowl of muesli?
A strong currant pulled him in!

Why was the turkey in the pop group?
Because he was the only one with drumsticks!

I'm reading a book on the history of glue –
I can't put it down!

Did you know?

UFO is short for an Unidentified Flying Object!

The sun is a star!

What did baby corn say to mama corn?

Where's Pop-corn?

What's the difference between an African elephant and an Indian elephant?

About 5000 miles!

What do you call a bear without ears?

B

What do hippopotamuses have that no other animals have?

Baby hippopotamuses!

Why do giraffes have long necks?
Because their feet smell!

What did the fish say when it swam into a wall?
Dam!

What's round and bad tempered?
A vicious circle!

On which side do chickens have the most feathers?
The outside!

What did the policeman say to the stomach?
You're under a vest!

What wobbles and flies?
A jelly-copter!

What goes ha, ha, ha clonk?
A man laughing his head off!

What athlete is warmest in winter?
A long jumper!

Did you hear about the kidnapping at school?
It's fine, he woke up!

Why'd the belt get arrested?
He held up a pair of pants!

Why would you invite a mushroom
to a party?
He's a *fun-guy* to be with!

What has four legs but can't walk?
A table!

Why did the hedgehog cross the road?
To see his *flat*-mate!

What kind of paper likes music?
Rapping paper!

What do you call a woman who stands between two goal posts?
Annette!

Did you hear about the man who bought a paper shop?
It blew away!

Did you know?

Ants are very strong for their size. Some ants can lift more than 100 times their own weight!

In England, during the 1880's, 'pants' was considered a dirty word!

What did the grape say when the elephant stepped on it?
Nothing. It just let out a little wine!

What do you call a belt with a watch on it?
A *waist* of time!

An invisible man marries an invisible woman and start a family.
The kids were not much to look at either!

This graveyard looks overcrowded. People must be *dying* to get in there!

Why move to Switzerland?
Well, the flag is a big plus!

Which country has the largest
appetite?
Hungary!

What do spacemen play in their spare time?
Astronauts and crosses!

How do you make an octopus laugh?
Ten tickles!

What do you call a zebra with no stripes?
A horse!

What do you get when you cross an elephant and a potato?
Mashed potatoes!

Would You Rather:

...be a pirate -or- a Viking?

Knock knock

.Who's there?

The interrupting bee.

The interrupting bee wh–

BUZZZZ!

Knock knock

.Who's there?

I'm in a loop.

I'm in a loop who?

Knock knock.

Knock knock.

Who's there?

Police.

Police who?

Hey! We are asking the questions here!

Why did the turkey cross the road?
Because he wasn't chicken!

What's orange and sounds like a parrot?
A carrot!

What do you call a blind dinosaur?
A do-you-think-he-saw-us!

Every time I stub my toe Dad asks, 'Should I call a *toe* truck?'

Did you know?

The United Kingdom's King George IV was so fat that he was given the nickname 'The Prince of Whales'.

Where do astronauts leave their cars?

At parking meteors!

Why are pines trees bad at sewing?

Because they are always dropping their needles!

Why can't a car play football?

Because they only have one boot!

Where do ghosts go swimming?

In the Dead Sea!

Would You Rather:

...be this guy

-or-

be this guy?

What does a frog do if his car
breaks down?
He gets it toad away!

What do you call a three-legged
donkey?
A wonky donkey!

How do hens encourage their
baseball teams?
They egg them on!

What tea do hockey players drink?
Penaltea!

Nostalgia isn't what it used to be!

Why can't a leopard hide?
Because they are always spotted!

Why is the cemetery such a noisy
place?
Because of all the *coffin!*

What do you get if you cross a
Christmas tree with an apple?
A pine-apple!

How do you organize a space
party?
You planet!

Why did the scarecrow win an
award?
**Because he was outstanding in his
field!**

Did you hear about the new
restaurant on the Moon?
**The food was great, but there was
just no atmosphere!**

Question:

What comes down but never goes up?

Answer:

Rain

I was thinking about moving to Moscow...
But there's no point in *Russian* into things!

What do you get when you cross a naughty sheep and a grumpy cow?
An animal that's in a baaaaaaaad mooooooood!

What do cows get when they're sick?
Hay fever!

How does a cow get to the moon?
It flies through udder space!

What do you call a monkey with a banana in each ear?
Anything you want, it can't hear you!

What did the buffalo say when his son left?
Bison!

How did the octopus beat a shark in a fight?
He was well armed!

A sandwich walks into a bar. Bartender says, "Sorry, we don't serve food here!"

Why did the pony need a glass of water?
He was a little *hoarse!*

You hear about the new broom?
It's sweeping the nation!

Velcro?
What a rip-off!

What do you call a man with a
rubber toe?
Roberto!

What do you call a fat psychic?
A four-chin teller!

I am terrified of elevators.
I'm going to start *taking steps* to
avoid them!

What do you call a cow you can't
see?
Ca-moo-flaged!

What do you call a bear with no teeth?

A gummy bear!

Why do you smear peanut butter on the road?

To go with the traffic jam!

What do you call the cat who was caught by the police?
The purrpetrator!

Why don't cats like online shopping?
They prefer cat-alogs!

What did the cat say when he lost his toys?
You got to be kitten me!

What happened to the lion who ate the comedian?
He felt funny!

Did you know?

A chameleon's tongue is twice the length of its body!

Saudi Arabia has no rivers!

What is a French cat's favorite
pudding?
Chocolate mousse!

Where do cows go for lunch?
The calf-eteria!

How many apples grow on a tree?
All of them!

What's a cat's favorite TV show?
The evening mews!

What looks like half a cat?
The other half!

Why did the old man fall in the well?

Because he couldn't see that well!

What did the dog say when he lost all his money?
I'm paw!

Want to hear a joke about paper?
Never mind, it's *tear-able*!

Why did the coffee file a police report?
It got mugged!

Want to hear a joke about construction?
I'm still working on it!

The shovel was a *ground-breaking* invention!

Did you know?

The T-Rex dinosaur went extinct 65 million years ago!

Did you know?

Moose have terribly poor vision!

111,111,111 x 111,111,111 =
12,345,678,987,654,321

Dad, can you put the cat out?
I didn't know it was on fire!

Cashier: 'Would you like the milk in
a bag?'
Dad: 'No, just leave it in the
carton!'

5/4 of people admit that they're
bad with fractions!

What do lawyers wear to court?
Lawsuits!

I used to work in a shoe recycling
shop.
It was *soul* destroying!

What five-letter word becomes shorter when you add two letters to it?

Short!

short + er

What do you get from a pampered cow?
Spoiled milk!

Two goldfish are in a tank. One says to the other, **"do you know how to drive this thing!?"**

My sister bet me that I couldn't make a car from spaghetti. **Later, after some time in the kitchen, I drove pasta!**

How many people live in South America?
A Brazilian!

How does a bear catch a fish
without a fishing pole?
With its *bear* hands!

I would avoid the sushi if I was
you.
It's a little fishy!

The *rotation* of Earth really makes my **day!**

I thought about going on an all cashew diet.
But that's just nuts!

Why do you never see elephants hiding in trees?
Because they're so good at it!

What is the highest form of flattery?
A plateau!

How does a penguin build its house?
Igloos it together!

Question:

What gets wetter as it dries?

Answer:

A towel

A Spanish magician says that he'll disappear on the count of three.
"Uno... dos..." POOF!
He disappeared without a *tres!*

I don't have to play soccer.
I'm just doing it for kicks!

Me: 'Hey, I was thinking...'
Dad: 'I thought I smelled something burning!'

How can you tell if an ant is a boy or a girl?
They're all girls, otherwise they'd be uncles!

I walked past a graveyard with my Dad and he said, 'Do you know why I can't be buried there?'
I asked, 'Why not?'
And Dad replies, '**Because I'm not dead yet!**'

What is Beethoven's favorite fruit?
A ba-na-na-na!

What did the pirate say on his 80th birthday?
Aye 'maighty!

What do you call a frozen dog?
A pup-sicle!

Why did the dog not want to play football?

It was a boxer!

Knock, knock.

Who's there?

Owls say

.Owls say who?

Yes, correct. Owls do say who.

I had a job at a calendar factory but I got the sack because I took a couple of *days off!*

I had a dream that I was a muffler last night. I woke up *exhausted!*

What did the right eye say to the left eye?
Between you and me, something smells!

What do you call a clever duck?
A wise quack!

Why do pandas like old movies?
Because they're in black and white!

4, 6, 8, and 9 have all been kidnapped,
2, 3, 5, 7, and 11 are the **prime suspects!**

What did one snowman say to the other one?
Do you smell carrots?

If your nose *runs* and your feet *smell*, you are built **upside down!**

Did you know?

A Roman emperor once planned to give his favorite horse the highest position in government!

Did you know?

The world's largest gold nugget weighed approximately 200 pounds!

Fingernails grow faster than toenails!

What's a teacher's favorite nation?
Expla-nation!

What do you call a cold dog?
A *chili* dog!

Where did the dog park his car?
In the *barking* lot!

What kind of key opens a banana?
A *mon-key!*

Why did the monkey like the banana?
Because it had *appeal!*

Would You Rather:

...have a big head
-or-
a small body?

Where do the chimps get their gossip?
On the *ape* vine!

How do baseball players stay cool?
They sit next to their fans!

What did Detective Duck say to his partner?
Let's quack this case!

Where did the duck go when he was sick?
To the ducktor!

What kind of shoes does a thief
wear?
Sneakers!

At what time does a duck wake
up?
At the quack of dawn!

What did the duck say when the
waitress came?
Put it on my bill!

How do ducks talk?
They don't, you quack!

What do you call a cow who plays
a musical instrument?
A moo-sician!

Knock knock.
Who's there?
Mustache.
Mustache who?
I mustache you a question.

What do you call a sheep with no legs?
A cloud!

What do you call a wet bear?
A drizzly bear!

Why don't bears like fast food?
Because they can't catch it!

What is a pirate's favorite store?
The second-hand store!

What has 8 eyes, 8 arms, & 8 legs?
Four rookie pirates!

How does a pirate clean his
house?
He has a yaaaaarrrrrd sale!

What's a pirate's favorite kind of
fish?
A gold-fish!

Did you know?

No two tigers have the same stripe pattern. Just like fingerprints they are unique!

Hippopotomonstrosesquipedaliophobia, is a fear of long words!

What's a chalkboard's favorite drink?
Hot chalk-olate!

Why did the student throw his watch out the window?
He wanted to see time fly!

Why shouldn't you do math in the jungle?
Because if you add 4+4 you get ate!

What happened to the plant in math class?
It grew square roots!

Would You Rather:

...own a crime-fighting police dog

-or-

own a crime-fighting hotdog?

What do a hockey player and a
magician have in common?
They both do hat tricks!

What can you serve but never
eat?
A volleyball!

Why did the chicken get sent off?
For fowl play!

What should a soccer team do if
the field is flooded?
Bring on their subs!

What's a tennis player's favorite city?
Volleywood!

Why did the students take ladders to school?
Because they were going to high school!

What's a runner's favorite subject at school?
Jog-raphy!

I don't trust atoms...
They make up everything!

Why can't you hear a pterodactyl
using the bathroom?
Because the P is silent!

What did one Japanese man say
to the other?
I don't know, I can't speak
Japanese!

What do you call a fake noodle?
An impasta!

Did you hear about the shampoo shortage in Jamaica?
It's dread-full!

Did you hear about the hungry clock?
It went back four seconds!

Me, 'Can I watch the TV?'
Dad, 'Yes, but don't turn it on!'

What did the mountain climber name his son?
Cliff!

Would You Rather:

...be a brightly-colored ninja

-or-

be a noisy ninja?

I went to buy some *camouflage* trousers the other day, but I couldn't **find** any!

Did you hear about the man who stole *a* calendar?
He got 12 months!

Which big cat was disqualified from the race?
The cheetah!

'Doctor, I've broken my arm in several places!'
'Well, don't go to those places.'

Did you know?

King Edward II of England attempted to ban soccer from being played!

The last letter added to the English alphabet was 'J'!

Slept like a log last night ... **woke up in the fireplace!**

A man woke up in a hospital after a serious accident.
He shouted, 'Doctor, I can't feel my legs!"
The doctor replied, 'I know you can't. **I've cut off your arms!'**

I knew I shouldn't have eaten that seafood.
Because now I'm feeling a little...
Eel!

What did the 0 say to the 8?
Nice belt!

'Ahh, this takes me back,' Dad says every time she reverses the car!

'Be careful standing near those trees.'
'Why?'
'They just look kind of shady to me!'

Where is the dead center of town?
The cemetery!

Would You Rather:

...kiss all the people you meet

-or-

kiss all the pets you meet?

Why couldn't the bike stand on its own?
Because it was *two tired*!

I don't trust stairs.
They're always up to something!

If a child refuses to take a nap, is he resisting *a rest?*

Want to hear my pizza joke?
Never mind, it's too cheesy!

What does a house wear?
A-ddress!

Did you know?

The sentence, 'The quick brown fox jumps over the lazy dog,' contains all the letters of the alphabet!

What is blue and doesn't weigh
very much?
Light blue!

They're finally making a film about
clocks...
It's about time!

I couldn't figure out why the
baseball kept getting larger. **Then
it hit me.**

What did the janitor say when he
jumped out of the closet?
Supplies!

I used to be afraid of hurdles...
Then I got over them!

My friend asked me to help him
round up his 37 sheep.
I said 40!

I have an addiction to cheddar
cheese...
But it's only mild!

What do you call a broken pencil?
Pointless!

Would You Rather:

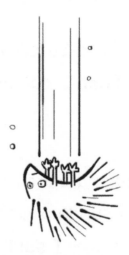

...catch a falling porcupine

-or-

pat an angry lion?

Did you hear about the magic tractor?
It was driving down the road and turned into a field!

I'm only familiar with 25 letters in the English language...
I don't know y!

Nothing rhymes with 'orange'.
No, it doesn't!

My friend recently got crushed by a pile of books...
But he has only got his shelf to blame!

Sometimes I tuck my knees into my chest and lean forward...
That's just how I roll!

What does a zombie vegetarian eat?
GRAAAAAINS!!!!

What vitamin helps your vision?
Vitamin C.

When do astronauts eat?
At launch time!

I once had dinner with a goat.
It wasn't baaaad.

What animal can jump higher than a house?

Most animals. A house can't jump!

What kind of bagel can fly?

A plain bagel!

Where do animals get new tails?

The retail store!

Two snare drums and a cymbal fall off a cliff..

BA-DUM tssshhh!

What sport do you play with a wombat?
Wom!

What do sea monsters eat?
Fish and ships!

Check out Silly Willy's other books!

If you loved this book, leave a review!

The End